Living with Cows

Living with Cows

BOB ARTLEY

IOWA STATE UNIVERSITY PRESS / AMES

For my wife, Margaret,

a constant help and inspiration in my work,

and one who, at an early age,

became acquainted with cows.

♾ Printed on acid-free paper in the United States of America

First edition, 1996

Library of Congress Cataloging-in-Publication Data

Artley, Bob
   Living with cows / Bob Artley.1st ed.
      p.   cm.
   "The material in this book is selected from the syndicated cartoon series, 'Memories of a former kid,' distributed by Extra Newspaper Features of Rochester, Minnesota, and Mug Wump Marketing of Hampton, Iowa"—P.
   ISBN 0-8138-2648-9 (alk. paper)
   1. Artley, Bob. 2. Cartoonists—Iowa—Biography. 3. Farm life—Iowa—Caricatures and cartoons. 4. American wit and humor, Pictorial. I. Title.
NC1429.A76A2   1996
741.5′973—dc20   96-32781

Last digit is the print number: 9 8 7 6 5 4 3 2 1

Contents

Acknowledgment

The material in this book is selected from the syndicated cartoon series, "Memories of a Former Kid," distributed by Extra Newspaper Features of Rochester, Minnesota, and Mug Wump Marketing of Hampton, Iowa, and appearing in publications throughout the country. In order to have a complete collection of Artley cartoons dealing with cows, this volume includes several drawings that have appeared in previous Bob Artley books: *Memories of a Former Kid, Cartoons,* and *Cartoons II.*

PREFACE

Just how far back in the mists of time the cow became an integral part of the human experience, I do not know. But I do know that my own experience with that wonderful creature began way back in *my* dim and distant past. For as long as I can remember cows and I were involved in a love-hate relationship that has had a lasting effect on me. One might say that I bonded with cows at an early age.

The contents of this book represent the entire gamut of emotions experienced by my brothers and me through our close association with the bovine herd on our farm during the 1920s and 30s. And, speaking for myself, cows are high on my list of our fellow creatures on this planet for which I feel genuine affection.

To this day, the warm friendly smell of a cow barn or cattle shed evokes in me nostalgia for a time and place where cows were very much a part of my growing-up years on our family farm.

Living with Cows

Mud

When Iowa Highway 10 (now 3), which crosses the state east and west about a mile south of our farm, was upgraded from gravel to concrete in the 1920s, Dad made the wistful comment that it would be nice to have just a small portion of all that paved surface in our cow yard.

This impossible dream was one that we all shared during the belly-deep mud days of the early spring thaws and the rainy seasons of spring and fall.

A spring-fed creek meandered through our pasture, making sloughs and mud holes that the cows frequented. They would seek out these soggy places in an attempt to escape the torment of biting flies that gathered on their legs and bellies. So when we brought the cows in for milking, it was necessary to clean their udders and the surrounding area in an effort to keep the milk clean.

The sloppy mixture of mud and manure in the cow yard in early spring caused us to think longingly of the frigid winter weather when the surface was frozen solid and the cows kept comparatively clean. Thus our joy in the first balmy days of spring was somewhat tempered by the prospect of muddy days that lay ahead.

THE FIRST "HONKERS" OF THE SEASON OFTEN COULD BE HEARD HIGH IN THE NIGHT SKY, AS THEY WINGED THEIR WAY NORTH.

10

WHEN THERE WAS A DIFFICULT BIRTH OF A CALF, IT WAS A TIME OF STRESS FOR ALL OF THOSE CONCERNED— IT TOOK ME A WHILE TO GET OVER IT.

ONE OF THE MOMENTOUS OCCASIONS OF SPRING— WHEN WE TURNED THE CATTLE OUT TO PASTURE FROM THE CONFINES OF THE MUDDY BARNYARD

19

27

Flies

When we were growing up on the farm, the shank of the summer (June, July, and August) was a wonderful time to be alive. But as so often is true of otherwise idyllic conditions, there was "a fly in the ointment."

This spoiler in our Garden of Eden was, to be sure, the fly—or more accurately, flies ... millions of them.

They bred in the ideal environment (for flies) of the manure piles around the barns and the cow patties in the pasture. The flies' eggs hatched into millions of maggots that soon evolved into flies. Even though the free-ranging chickens scratched in these manure piles and fed upon the maggots and grubs they found there, they made no appreciable decrease in the fly population.

One of the great variety of fly species that were generated in these natural incubators was one slightly smaller than a housefly that we called a cowfly. This voracious blood-sucker had a mean bite and was the biggest problem for our bovine co-inhabitants of the cow barn—for cow and herder alike. They covered the backs, sides, bellies, legs, and faces of the poor creatures and made life miserable for them as they bit and sucked their blood.

The only defenses the cows had against their tormentors were their switching tails and to stand in water and mud in close-packed herds.

All of this preoccupation with biting flies cut down on the milk production and could make the process of extracting it a bad experience for cow as well as milker, who had to deal with flailing tails and or kicking hooves.

We tried to mitigate the suffering for all concerned by using various patented fly sprays on the cows when we brought them into the barn, or by wiping them down with a rag soaked in the spray solution. At best, this was only a temporary relief, but it was another incentive (in addition to seeking relief from a full udder) that brought the often stubborn critters into their stanchions willingly.

Mostly, fly time was a time to endure.

32

33

34

36

37

38

40

41

43

45

46

49

51

Corn

When the scent of green corn announced the presence of ears maturing on the stalks, the cattle seemed to be the first to pick up the message. What had formerly seemed to be a gentle herd of cows grazing contentedly in a peaceful pasture suddenly changed into restless animals with a far-away look in their eyes.

If the pasture bordered on a cornfield, our own or a neighbor's, the fence between had better be a sturdy one, for the cows would patrol up and down the length of it, reaching through for the corn and testing the fence for its weakest place. Up until the invention of the electric fence, mere barbed wire didn't seem to be much of a deterrence in keeping the corn-obsessed cows from plunging right on through to feed on the succulent ears, leaves, and stalks.

Thus it was not unusual during the roasting-ear stage of the corn's development, when going to fetch the cows at milking time, to find the pasture deserted and a section of fence flattened or broken over and evidence of stripped and trodden-down cornstalks at the site.

"The cows are in the corn," was a dreaded alarm call that could shatter the peace of a summer day.

In addition to having to round up the errant critters and get them back into the pasture, it often meant opening another stretch of fence, since they'd forgotten the hole they'd made. The fence then had to be repaired—either replacing broken-off wooden posts or straightening bent-over steel ones.

Invariably at least one of the wayward cows had sustained a wire cut or two. If a teat had been slashed, milking was made more difficult when it was grasped and pulled to extract the milk. The discomfort often caused the cow to respond by a violent kick.

There was hardly a summer that went by that we didn't experience the touchy task of squeezing milk from a very sore teat on a cow that seemed to have forgotten how she got the cut. And by next corn season, if not before, she was eager to get into the corn again.

57

59

60

63

65

66

67

70

71

Cold Hands

During the winter months there was always the problem of keeping our hands and feet from getting frostbite while doing chores around the farmyard.

On our feet we wore one or two pairs of heavy wool socks, leather work shoes, and a pair of four- or five-buckle, flannel-lined overshoes. We would swing and stamp our feet in an effort to keep the blood circulating. But even with all of those efforts, long before we had finished trudging back and forth through the snow and ice of the barnyard, our toes became like balls of ice and we looked longingly to when we could go into the house and soak our bare feet in a pan of tepid water, hoping to avert frostbite and resulting chilblains.

Our hands were covered by at least two pairs of cotton flannel mittens. But even so, after an hour of grasping the icy handles of forks and scoop shovels and the bails of buckets as we dipped them into the ice-fringed water of the stock tank, carrying water to the pigs, chickens and calves, our fingers were tingling or aching with the cold.

Thus it was that we looked forward to our trip into the cow

barn when we could warm our hands on the warm udders and teats of the milk cows.

This fringe benefit of milking by hand must have been anything but pleasant for the poor cows. They would often start slightly and each would turn her head and look at me with a doleful eye, when upon first sitting down to milk I'd slip my cold hands up into the warm pockets formed between the full udder and soft flanks.

75

77

83

84

85

87

89

94

95